The Story of Christmas

bookoli

Many years ago, a young woman called Mary lived happily in the little town of Nazareth.

Mary would soon be married to Joseph. He was a carpenter and worked hard to make wonderful things out of wood.

One sunny day, while Mary
was in her garden, a white light
shone down.

It was the Angel Gabriel!

"You will soon have a very special baby boy," the angel told Mary. "He will be the Son of God. You will call him Jesus."

Mary and Joseph were filled with happiness! They soon got married and waited for their little baby to be born.

Before the baby was due, Mary and Joseph were ordered to go to Bethlehem to add their names to a list.

Mary felt tired, but she slowly got ready for their journey.

They walked and walked for many miles and many days. It was a slow journey on a long and dusty road.

"I am too tired to walk," sighed poor Mary, so Joseph found a donkey for her to ride on.

The gentle animal carried its heavy load with care.

When Mary and Joseph finally arrived in Bethlehem, there were people everywhere.

"I'm sorry, there is no room at the inn," said the innkeeper. But seeing that Mary was about to have a baby, the innkeeper wanted to help.

"You can stay in the stable,"
he said, kindly.

Mary was happy to have somewhere to rest at last.

That night, snuggled up in the warm stable, baby Jesus was born!

"Thank you, God, for this precious gift," Mary said, gently placing Jesus in a manger.

High in the sky, a new star appeared. It shone brightly down over the stable.

Up on the hills of Bethlehem, a group of shepherds sat watching over their flock.

Suddenly, in a magical blaze of light, an angel flew down from the sky.

"I bring wonderful news! The Son of God has been born!" the angel told the shepherds. "You will find him in a manger."

The shepherds couldn't believe it! They searched Bethlehem until they finally found baby Jesus. "Praise the Lord!" they gasped in joy.

The special news spread fast.
"The Son of God is here! The Son of God is here!" the shepherds told everybody they passed.

Far away in the East, three Wise Men spotted the new star.
It shone more brightly than all the other stars in the sky.

They knew right away that it was a very special star, one that meant a new king had been born.

The magical star guided the Wise Men all
the way to the stable in Bethlehem.

They slowly knelt before the new king and offered him gifts.
"We have brought you gold, frankincense and myrrh, our Lord,"
the Wise Men said.

When all of their visitors had gone and it was quiet in the stable once again, Mary and Joseph gazed down at baby Jesus.

They knew he was a very special boy.
"You are going to save the world,"
Mary whispered.

The Son of God had been born on Christmas Day.